# SELF-COMPASSION JOURNAL
## FOR
## FIRST-TIME MOMS

# SELF-COMPASSION JOURNAL

## FOR

# FIRST-TIME MOMS

### PROMPTS AND PRACTICES TO NURTURE KINDNESS AND SELF-CARE

HANNA G. KREINER, LICSW

ROCKRIDGE
PRESS

For general information on our other products and services or to obtain technical support, please contact our Customer Care Department within the United States at (866) 744-2665, or outside the United States at (510) 253-0500.

Rockridge Press publishes its books in a variety of electronic and print formats. Some content that appears in print may not be available in electronic books, and vice versa.

TRADEMARKS: Rockridge Press and the Rockridge Press logo are trademarks or registered trademarks of Callisto Media Inc. and/or its affiliates, in the United States and other countries, and may not be used without written permission. All other trademarks are the property of their respective owners. Rockridge Press is not associated with any product or vendor mentioned in this book.

Interior and Cover Designer: Tricia Jang
Art Producer: Janice Ackerman
Editor: Brian Sweeting
Production Manager: Michael Kay
Production Editor: Melissa Edeburn

Author photo: Lydia Brewer Photography
Illustration: Courtesy of Creative Market

Paperback ISBN: 978-1-63807-419-9

R0

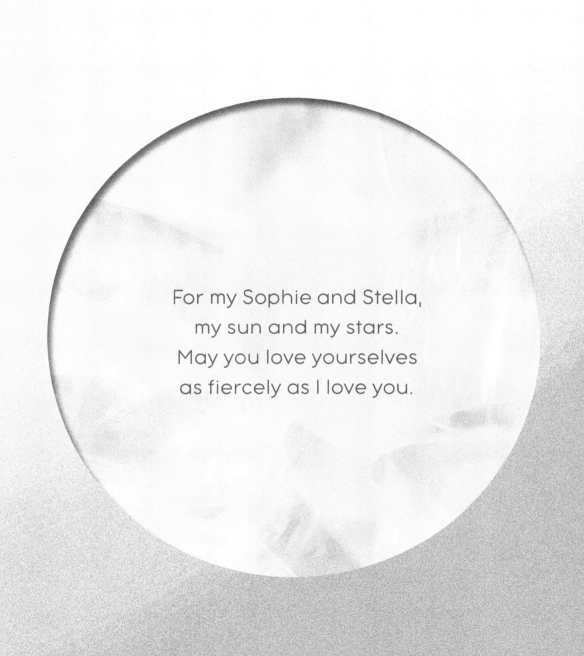

For my Sophie and Stella,
my sun and my stars.
May you love yourselves
as fiercely as I love you.

# CONTENTS

# INTRODUCTION

"You yourself, as much as anybody in the entire universe, deserve your love and affection."

–SHARON SALZBERG

HOLY MOLY! YOU'RE A MOM! Congratulations, and welcome to the Mom Club. It's the best club you'll ever join, with a lifetime membership, major perks, and what some might call . . . dues. I'm so glad you're here.

This journal is for *all* moms—whether you birthed your baby, used surrogacy, adopted, or are a stepmom, you belong here. What you'll find in these pages is more indispensable to moms than anything in your diaper bag: self-compassion. Compassion is the feeling of being moved by someone else's struggle and wanting to help. Self-compassion is turning that feeling toward oneself in times of difficulty. Essentially, it's caring for ourselves the way we care for our friends.

If there's any question why a first-time mom may need self-compassion, allow me to state the obvious: This is a huge moment of transformation in your life, and change is hard! In fact, the process you're in has a name: "matrescence," coined by Dana Raphael, PhD, in 1973. It's the name for the physical, emotional, mental, and identity-shifting transition of becoming a mother. It began when you started thinking about becoming a parent, continues to evolve well after you have your baby, and recurs with each new child. Matrescence is a healthy developmental milestone, like adolescence, marked by exciting and uncomfortable changes in your body, brain, relationships, and more.

We wouldn't need compassion if motherhood were all joy. I am a mother of two, and I know firsthand that motherhood is truly awesome–and constantly demanding. The nonstop vigilance can be overwhelming: *Is the baby breathing? Are they eating enough? Are they cold/hot/hungry/tired? Am I doing this right?* When you finally get a moment for yourself, you usually have to decide between essentials like sleeping, eating, or showering. It's a rarity to feel rested, nourished, and refreshed in the same day. And, of course, when you finally get into a groove, everything changes! On top of the demands of getting through each day as a new family, first-time moms often worry about the potential long-term impacts of their countless decisions. From feeding to primary childcare, opinions about what is "best" for the baby abound.

It's easy to get caught up in self-doubt as you figure out the right path for your unique family and circumstances.

How you respond to these relentless challenges will shape how you feel and relate to yourself in this new role. As a psychotherapist, social worker, and mindfulness teacher, I have worked with people dealing with serious illnesses, mental health issues, and life's biggest transitions. Often the most painful parts of their experiences are the added burdens of their self-judgment, feeling permanently defined by their hardship, and feeling isolated. Self-compassion is the balm for these stresses; it offers the skills of being kind to ourselves in the midst of struggle, seeing ourselves and our situation clearly, and recognizing and connecting to our common humanity. These are skills anyone can learn; it just takes practice. You can meet your multifaceted transformation into motherhood, empowered with tools to be both tender and fierce in caring for yourself.

This journal can help you learn and practice self-compassion by engaging with writing prompts, exercises, affirmations, and quotes. Just showing up to this journal is an act of self-compassion. You're very busy right now, so do what feels helpful to you. It's okay if you don't finish every prompt. Self-compassion is a lifelong practice and will deepen as you and your family evolve. Take your time exploring the writing prompts and exercises in these pages, and return to them often to sustain yourself. Journaling through this time of adjustment and growth will lay the foundation for an integrated and more peaceful experience of being a mom. Please keep in mind that this journal is a complement to, and not a substitute for, a therapist, medication, or medical treatment if needed. Postpartum mood disorders are common and highly treatable. There is no shame in seeking help—it is the self-compassionate thing to do.

In this process of becoming a mother, your heart is growing and opening to your little one, and to the seismic shift in who you are. Take this opportunity of growth to include yourself in the circle of loved ones you care for, nourish, and protect. Your child's mother (you!) deserves kindness and acceptance. This is a chance to practice self-care simply because you are worthy of care. This work is important. Place a hand on your heart and say to yourself, "This one matters, too."

LET'S BEGIN.

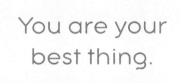

You are your
best thing.

−TONI MORRISON

# START WHERE YOU ARE

From the first heart-expanding moment you laid eyes on your child, everything changed. You became a mom. You are still you, but you are changing, too. This is your first time being a mom, and it's a lot to navigate!

This section is about practicing compassion. The following exercises will help you see yourself just as you are and the situation just as it is—without assumptions from the past or fears of the future but instead with curiosity and the notion that nothing needs to be "fixed." When we see things more clearly, we are more flexible, kind, and forgiving.

You don't have to wait to start being kind to yourself. Where you are now is the perfect place to begin.

## GET COMFORTABLE!

The first weeks and months of caring for a baby are physically challenging. Your body may be recovering from pregnancy, labor and delivery, surgery, and the excitement and stress of your baby's arrival. Some moms may be breastfeeding or pumping, and everyone is sleep-deprived. As we hold our babies, we often wrap our bodies around our precious ones, rounding our shoulders and stretching our necks down to gaze lovingly. This all takes a physical toll, and self-compassion includes being kind to your body.

Take a moment now to offer yourself warmth, support, and comfort. Use pillows behind your back and neck, find a soft blanket, put on fuzzy socks, make yourself a cup of tea—or do anything else that sounds good for you.

Everytime you open this journal ask yourself, "How can I be even 5 percent more comfortable?" Doing so makes a difference!

# WARM WELCOME

Once you're very comfortable and cozy, sit in a supported position, place a hand on your heart, and take a few deep breaths. You are here now. Your presence is all that's required. Now, welcome yourself to this moment and this journal process in a warm and friendly way. Smile as if seeing a dear friend. Write your greeting; it may be as simple as saying to yourself, "Welcome, [your name]. I'm glad you're here." Write whatever feels kind and genuine to you.

_____

_____

_____

_____

_____

_____

_____

_____

# REFLECTION

How does it feel to welcome yourself and to offer the same warmth to yourself as you would to someone you love dearly? Can you offer and receive this kindness and friendliness? If not, what do you notice? Can you be kind and open to whatever it is that you are feeling? Write your reflection here.

_____

_____

_____

_____

_____

_____

_____

_____

_____

# A SUPPORTED START

Your comfort and safety will allow you to get the most out of this journal. What can you do to ensure that you feel safe enough to open up in this process? Is it privacy? The support of someone to talk to about what you discover? Write a few sentences about what can set you up for success with this journal.

_____

_____

_____

_____

_____

_____

_____

_____

_____

# WHAT BRINGS YOU HERE?

You've taken the step of opening this journal about nurturing kindness and acceptance. What does that mean to *you?* Use this space to explore the questions below. I encourage you to be really honest and vulnerable with yourself as you write.

Why am I here? _____

_____

_____

_____

_____

Why now? _____

_____

_____

_____

_____

## MINDFUL CHECK-INS

How can you be there for yourself if you don't even know how you're doing?

    In the next three exercises, you'll pause to notice how you're feeling in your mind, body, and heart. When you're done with each check-in, write what you noticed.

## MINDFUL MIND

Sit comfortably and take a deep breath. Pay attention to what's happening in your mind as if you're an observer. Notice if your mind is full of thoughts, if it feels like it's moving quickly or slowly, or if it appears clear or cloudy. Perhaps several thoughts are moving through, or one or two thoughts are circling around. Notice how thoughts come and go—you don't need to follow them. See if you can witness your mindstate without judging it. Allow whatever is here to be here. If images arise as you do this check-in, allow them to take shape. Turn your attention inward. Then, write your reflections here.

_____

_____

_____

_____

## MINDFUL BODY

Notice what's happening in your body right now. Scan your body from head to toe with kind awareness of physical sensations. You may notice tension or ease, heaviness, lightness, warmth or coolness, movement, vibrations, or other sensations. Notice whether the sensations change as you pay attention. Observe what's happening inside with curiosity. With mindfulness, none of these sensations are good or bad; they simply are. Allow whatever is here to be here. If images arise, allow them. Close your eyes, turn your attention inside, and check in now. Write your reflections here.

_____

_____

_____

_____

_____

_____

_____

## MINDFUL HEART

Notice what's happening in your heart and what emotions are present. Emotions may be tied to physical sensations and thoughts. See if you can label the feelings (sad, happy, excited, disappointed, etc.) without judging them as good or bad. Allow whatever is here to be here. Notice if the feelings change in intensity as you pay attention with curiosity. If images arise as you do this check-in, allow them to take shape. Take a moment to close your eyes, turn your attention inside, and check in now with kindness. Write your reflections here.

_____

_____

_____

_____

_____

_____

With practice, these three check-ins (mind, body, and heart) can be done simultaneously to achieve clarity.

# HEY, BABE!

When we talk regularly to people we love, like our babies, it's common to use affectionate nicknames, or pet names, to address them. Did you know you could talk to yourself this way? Make a list of potential nicknames you could use for yourself that make you feel good. These could be what others call you already, what you call others you love, or something completely new and just for you. You got this, Mama!

_____

_____

_____

_____

_____

_____

_____

_____

# YOU DID IT!

You have a baby! What a journey to get here! Can you offer yourself kindness for that process? Write a brief letter of appreciation to yourself for what you have experienced to get to this point. Everyone has their unique path to parenthood. What was that journey like for you?

_____

_____

_____

_____

_____

_____

_____

_____

Self-compassion is a crucial practice for parents. If we continually give to others without nurturing ourselves, our emotional gas tank will be stuck on empty. By nurturing and supporting ourselves, we will have more emotional resources to give to our children.

–KIM FREDRICKSON

# NICE TO MEET YOU, LITTLE ONE

You are your baby's mom. It's arguably the most meaningful relationship there is. Just as you're learning about your baby, they're learning about you, too. Write a letter to your baby introducing yourself. Say something about who you were before they arrived, and who you hope to be. Include at least three qualities you appreciate about yourself.

_____

_____

_____

_____

_____

_____

_____

_____

_____

# WHAT MAKES A GOOD MOM?

We receive mothering from many sources in our lives. Reflect on your relationships with the people who have shaped your life for the better. What did they do that made a positive impact on you, and how did they make you feel?

_____

_____

_____

_____

_____

Do you, or could you, see those qualities in yourself?

_____

_____

_____

_____

_____

# WHAT DOESN'T MATTER

Referring to the previous prompt, what is *not* on that list? Did the mother figures in your life need to look a certain way, or have their homes look just so? What do you realize was not needed to be a good or great mom?

_____

_____

_____

_____

_____

_____

_____

_____

_____

# I AM . . .

How would your loved ones describe you? List at least five positive qualities others see in you. How your loved ones see you is valid. As you write your list, remind yourself that you really are all these things, and more.

1. _____

2. _____

3. _____

4. _____

5. _____

## COMFORTING TOUCH

When we're stressed, we need tools that help right away. Physical touch soothes our nervous systems and helps us release feel-good hormones such as oxytocin. We all need touch, but as a new mom, your preferences for physical contact may be changing. Your contact with your baby may be restorative or sometimes uncomfortable. Some new moms talk about being "touched out" and not wanting to be touched by others at all. You know best what you need, which means you can offer yourself touch that feels supportive and comforting.

Try out the following gentle gestures on yourself, taking a few breaths with each, and see how they feel for you:

* One or two hands on your heart

* One or two hands on your belly

* Resting your cheek in one palm

* Holding your face between both palms

* Hugging yourself

Try these gestures again while moving your hands in small circles or up and down. Notice how movement and warmth change the experience for you.

# REFLECTION

How does it feel to offer yourself some comforting touch? Are there gestures that feel kind and supportive for you? Do they remind you of other times you have felt comforted or soothed another? Is there another gesture that feels more comfortable and that you can infuse with compassion for yourself?

_____

_____

_____

_____

_____

_____

_____

_____

# CHALLENGES & WINS

Make a list of some of the challenging aspects of life as a new mom. Can you match each with something that's going well? Remember to include what *you* are doing well in your list of highlights.

CHALLENGES

1. _____
2. _____
3. _____
4. _____
5. _____

WINS

1. _____
2. _____
3. _____
4. _____
5. _____

# WHAT DO YOU NEED?

The fundamental question of self-compassion is *What do I need?* From the challenges you wrote about, and from your other experiences as a new mom, what do you need? A lot of us could use more hours in the day, but try to write about things that are in the realm of possibility—such as having more help with certain tasks or time for yourself to do something meaningful. Write a few sentences about what you need right now.

_____

_____

_____

_____

_____

_____

_____

_____

## THREE-PART BREATH

Place one hand on your chest and one hand on your belly. As you breathe in, expand your belly, then your ribs, then your chest. Then breathe out, allowing the exhale to relax your chest, then ribs, then belly. Make it as effortless as possible. Breathe like this for five complete cycles, focusing solely on your breath. Return to your breath when your mind wanders. Record any thoughts that arise.

_____

_____

_____

_____

_____

_____

_____

_____

# WHAT'S YOUR STRESS STORY?

When you think about your biggest motherhood challenges so far, what stories do you find you're telling yourself? Are these stories absolutely true? Are you blaming yourself unfairly? Are you saying absolutes like "always" and "never"?

_____

_____

_____

_____

_____

_____

_____

_____

# KIND WORDS

Offer yourself some kind words. From the needs you identified (on page 20), create a few wishes for yourself (for example, *May I be supported, May I feel rested*). You can write "May I . . ." or just the wish on its own. By writing these goodwill wishes, you're offering yourself some kindness and compassion.

* _____

* _____

* _____

* _____

* _____

## AWWW!

Have you noticed how you respond to your baby when they're upset? Do you offer some sort of "Awww" or "Ohhh" sound? Many people automatically use a gentle tone of voice as they talk with babies. Research shows that this tone is hardwired in humans to foster connection and feelings of safety (Steller and Keltner, 2014). When we speak to ourselves with a gentle tone and offer a genuine "Awww" to ourselves when we're struggling, we release stress. It may feel awkward at first, but try it right now! Place a hand on your heart for extra comfort. Awww! Ohhh!

# EVERYDAY SELF-COMPASSION

Make a list of five compassionate things you can do for yourself on a regular basis. They can be as simple as getting enough to eat, petting the dog, or texting a friend. Take a photo of this list and make it the background of your phone, or post it where you'll see it often. This list will serve as a reminder to do something kind for yourself every day.

1. _____

2. _____

3. _____

4. _____

5. _____

I AM COMMITTED
TO LEARNING
AND GROWING
AS A MOM,
*AND* I LOVE MYSELF
JUST AS I AM.

Being human is not hard
because you're doing it wrong,
it's hard because you're doing it right.
You will never change the fact that
being human is hard, so you must
change your idea that it was
ever supposed to be easy.

–GLENNON DOYLE

# EMBRACE YOUR EMOTIONS

We all want to feel kind, loving, and peaceful 24/7, but you may have noticed that being a mom is complicated! As a new mom, you may feel overwhelming joy one moment and deep dread the next. Excitement, sadness, worry, resentment, anger, jealousy, and the whole spectrum of emotions are completely normal, especially during such a major life transition. Sometimes you may not even know what you're feeling.

Self-compassion offers a way to connect deeply to all parts of our experience. Self-compassion is the practice of bringing kindness to all your (very valid) emotions. This section will help you become more mindful and accepting of your feelings as you adjust to your new role as Mom. Learning to embrace the range of your emotions will help you love yourself throughout the ups and downs of parenthood.

## BODY SCAN

We call emotions feelings because we *feel* them! A body scan can help us identify and familiarize ourselves with our feelings.

Start with some comforting touch, like a hand on your heart, to signal that you care for your body. When you're ready, lie down, close your eyes, and imagine taking a tour of your body.

Check from head to toe, nonjudgmentally describing to yourself what you feel (temperature, ease, aches, movement) with curiosity and kindness.

TIP: Guided practice recordings can be found in the Resources section (page 154).

# SURPRISE!

Motherhood is full of surprises. What have you found surprising so far? As you write, think about assumptions you had before becoming a mom. By noticing the differences between expectations and what came to be, you can practice being present in the adventure of parenting.

_____

_____

_____

_____

_____

_____

_____

_____

_____

## HOW ARE YOU?

No, really, how *are* you? We are complex beings capable of feeling a wide range of emotions—sometimes many at once. Below, circle any and all of the feelings you have experienced since becoming a mom. This is a no-judgment zone! All these feelings and more are a normal part of being human and a mother.

| | | | |
|---|---|---|---|
| Joyful | Peaceful | Hurt | Powerless |
| Happy | Loving | Isolated | Criticized |
| Excited | Satisfied | Lonely | Mad |
| Grateful | Appreciated | Grief | Irritated |
| Trusting | Tender | Disappointed | Ambivalent |
| Confident | Sad | Discouraged | Defensive |
| Connected | Depressed | Regretful | Vulnerable |
| Impatient | Afraid | Ashamed | Frustrated |
| Panicked | Resentful | Disrespected | Worried |
| Guilty | Confused | Lost | Incompetent |
| Numb | Anxious | Disgusted | Infuriated |
| Playful | Insecure | Surprised | Betrayed |

## WHAT TO DO WITH HARD FEELINGS

Bring to mind a time you struggled after becoming a mom. (Try not to choose an intensely difficult moment while you're learning self-compassion.) Imagine the struggle clearly—what happened, who was there, and what was done, said, or thought. The following three practices will help you bring self-compassion to this experience.

## 1. NAME IT TO TAME IT

Using the feeling list in the table presented earlier, and adding any of your own, write out all the emotions you felt in the moment of difficulty. This simple act of labeling how you felt (and feel) can help you recognize what's happening inside, and this cultivates more calm.

_____

_____

_____

_____

_____

# 2. FEEL IT TO HEAL IT

Thinking of that memory again and the difficult emotion(s), notice how your body feels.

What do you feel, and where in your body do you feel it? Try to use descriptive words as you notice any sensations (tension, warmth, pulsing, constriction), and imagine making space for these sensations to be here. Your intention is to allow them to be here even though the feelings may be unpleasant and difficult.

Keep breathing steadily as you feel what's inside, and notice if anything changes.

Write a few sentences about what you experienced in your body as you felt the challenging emotion. Did it change as you acknowledged the sensations?

_____

_____

_____

_____

_____

_____

_____

# 3. SPEAK KINDLY TO YOURSELF

Try writing some kind, acknowledging words to your body about the difficulty it's feeling. (*I can see you're hurting. It's okay to feel this discomfort. May I be kind to myself.*) Include some of the well wishes from your Kind Words practice (page 23).

_____

_____

_____

_____

_____

_____

_____

_____

# 4. LISTENING TO YOUR EMOTIONS

Our emotions are here to guide us and give us important information, often about what we need. What are the feelings that you explored in the previous practices trying to tell you?

_____

_____

_____

_____

_____

_____

_____

_____

_____

_____

## GET GROUNDED

There's *so* much to think about as a first-time mom that you can easily lose touch with the moment. Feeling grounded means being present in your body and aware of your connection to the earth.

Notice how your body is supported right now. Are you sitting, standing, or lying down? Pay attention to where your body meets the chair, bed, or floor. Can you relax the part of you that is being held from beneath?

You are here right now, and in this moment, everything is okay.

You can repeat this practice anytime, anywhere, when you feel overwhelmed.

Happiness stems from loving ourselves and our lives exactly as they are, knowing that joy and pain, strength and weakness, glory and failure are all essential to the full human experience.

—KRISTIN NEFF

# HAPPINESS LIVES HERE

Bring to mind a time when you felt really, truly happy as a new mom. What does your body feel like when you're happy? You might notice a smile, warmth in your face, a lightness in your chest, or something else. When we allow difficult feelings, we feel our positive emotions more profoundly. Write down what happiness feels like in you to help you recognize and savor the experience.

_____

_____

_____

_____

_____

_____

_____

_____

# THERE ARE USUALLY
# BUMPS IN THE ROAD

Things often don't go as we hope or plan from the moment we decide to have a baby. Have you experienced any disappointments in your motherhood journey so far?

_____

_____

_____

_____

   What kind words or comforting touch can you offer yourself regarding these disappointments?

_____

_____

_____

_____

# OH, BABY!

Babies cry. It's a fact. To hear *your* baby cry touches a distinct, and often painful, place inside a mother's heart. How do you feel when your baby cries? Is there anything you do to care for yourself in those moments (e.g., deep breaths, comforting touch, telling yourself and your baby you're both okay)?

_____

_____

_____

_____

_____

_____

_____

_____

_____

# OH, MAMA!

Moms cry, too! Have you cried with joy, sorrow, or frustration? How do you feel when you cry? Are you able to allow tears to flow when they come?

_____

_____

_____

_____

What have you learned so far from this journal that might help you care for yourself? Is there anything you can tell yourself in those moments (e.g., It's okay to cry; I'm doing the best I can)?

_____

_____

_____

_____

## SELF-COMPASSION BREAK

TIP: Guided practice recordings can be found in the Resources section (page 154).

(This exercise has been adapted from Kristin Neff's "Self-Compassion Break.")

This practice helps you be self-compassionate in a moment of struggle. Think of a time you struggled since becoming a mom. It could be a feeling you had, something stressful that happened, or a difficult interaction. (Try to choose something only mildly to moderately difficult.) Imagine the struggle clearly—what happened, who was there, and what was done, said, or thought. Now follow the steps below.

1. Be mindful that this is a moment of struggle. Say to yourself, "This is hard," "I'm hurting right now," or, "I wish things were different, and that's painful."

2. Connect to our shared humanity and experience of motherhood. Say, "This is what it feels like to be a mom," "Other moms go through this, too," or, "I'm not alone."

3. Be kind to yourself. Offer yourself some comforting touch and kind words. Say, "May I be kind to myself during this struggle," "I deserve forgiveness/love/peace," or, "I can do this. I am strong."

Take these steps whenever you're hurting.

# IT'S OKAY TO VENT

New moms face so many new challenges in rapid succession, all while sleep-deprived and adjusting to their complex roles as Mom. Yet new moms often hesitate to talk about difficulties for fear they'll be seen as "complaining" or ungrateful. It's OKAY to let it all out here. What would you add to this sentence? "I'm so grateful, and . . ."

_____

_____

_____

_____

_____

_____

_____

_____

# MOMS HAVE FEELINGS, TOO

You and your baby are developing a deep relationship. Write a letter to your baby telling them how you're feeling lately.  Share any feelings of joy, gratitude, and connection. Also share what's feeling tough for you. These are your feelings, and they are natural to have, so practice speaking about difficulty without blaming anyone, including yourself and your baby. Speak in the first person, and use simple and honest language.

_____

_____

_____

_____

_____

_____

_____

# SPEAK FREELY

New moms often hear, "Enjoy this time!" and, "It goes so fast." What would you like to say in response?

_____

_____

_____

_____

_____

_____

_____

_____

_____

## STRESS DOODLE

When you can't find the words to express the stress you feel as a mom, draw it here:

# TWO MINUTES OF GRATITUDE

Time yourself for two minutes, and make a list of what you're grateful for as a mom. Be super specific. Writing for two minutes may encourage you to think beyond the "big" things and notice the "small" things that still make a big difference in your life.

_____

_____

_____

_____

_____

_____

_____

_____

_____

## JOY DOODLE

When you can't find the words to express the joy you feel as a mom, draw it here:

## SHAKE IT OFF!

When feelings get intense, your body craves movement. Stand up and shake your arms, your legs, your body, and your head. As you move, imagine you're able to move the feelings around, process them, and release them. It may look silly, but it will feel great!

# REMEMBER SLEEP?

Rest and sleep have a major impact on our general mood and how we cope with stress. How is the disruption in your sleep affecting you? Is there anything that might help you get more rest or feel more rested? Write about your reflections and ideas here.

_____

_____

_____

_____

_____

_____

_____

_____

# ALLOWING THE HARD STUFF

Having difficult feelings is a natural part of being human. Even if you don't embrace your emotions, can you allow them to be part of your experience? Write about what would happen if you were more accepting of your difficult feelings.

_____

_____

_____

_____

_____

_____

_____

_____

_____

_____

_____

I WILL ALLOW MYSELF
TO EXPERIENCE THE
WHOLENESS OF
MOTHERHOOD AND ALL
ITS COMPLEX FEELINGS
WITHOUT JUDGMENT.
THIS WILL MAKE
ME A MORE PRESENT
AND AUTHENTIC PERSON
AND MOM.

When someone says
to us, as Thich Nhat Hanh
suggests, "Darling, I care
about your suffering,"
a deep healing begins.

—TARA BRACH

# SPEAK TO YOURSELF LIKE A FRIEND

You can do this! Self-compassion may feel totally new, but you've been practicing how to be compassionate in your relationships with others for a long time. As a friend, and now as a mom, you have listened to, encouraged, and comforted others you care for countless times. These are skills you already have that you can offer yourself, too!

In this section, we'll explore how you can include yourself in the compassion you naturally give to people you care about. You're just as deserving of love and understanding as everyone else. A compassionate voice is inside us all, able to care for ourselves even better than anyone else could—it just needs practice. Our work together is to invite that voice to speak up for ourselves and be heard.

# BE A FRIEND TO YOURSELF

Bring to mind a situation that led to feelings of hardship, inadequacy, or disconnection for you as a new mom. It could be about feeding your baby, relating to your partner or family, how your body is feeling, or some other stress. Try to focus on something mildly difficult and not the most intense challenge you've faced. Remember what happened, who was there, and how you felt.

Now recall what you said to yourself in the face of this hardship. What kind of tone did you use with yourself?

_____

_____

_____

Think of one of your close friends. Imagine they went through a similar situation and told you about it. What would you say to your friend, and how would you say it?

_____

_____

_____

_____

What differences do you notice between how you talk to yourself and how you talk to a friend?

_____

_____

_____

Would you say to others what you say to yourself? What would happen if you did?

_____

_____

_____

What do you make of the differences between how you talk to yourself and how you talk to a friend?

_____

_____

_____

# WHAT WOULD YOUR
# BEST FRIEND SAY?

Remembering the same difficult situation, can you imagine what one of your best friends would say to you? Write out what you think they would say and how. Then reflect on what it's like to hear some friendly support, realizing that these words really came from *you*.

_____

_____

_____

_____

_____

_____

_____

_____

## FRIENDLY BREATH

Sit upright and relaxed, and bring a hand to rest on your body where it feels comforting. Notice the warmth of your hand on yourself, and smile as you welcome yourself to this moment. Focus on what it feels like to breathe in and out.

Imagine breathing in love and breathing out peace. Say "love" to yourself on the inhale, and "peace" on the exhale.

Practice for at least one minute, and notice how you feel.

# KEEPING IT REAL

Sometimes the best thing a friend says at first is not a suggestion or encouragement but a simple statement acknowledging, "That sucks." Saying it like it is *is* a way to be mindful! These are phrases we can say to ourselves to acknowledge and validate disappointments and difficulties. Write about a time when a friend was there for you with validation.

_____

_____

_____

_____

What phrases resonate with you when something bad has happened?

_____

_____

_____

_____

# YOU'RE NOT ALONE

When we're struggling, it is so helpful to remember that we're not the only ones to feel this way, and we're not "wrong" or "bad" for experiencing difficulty (even if we did make a mistake). Some might say, "People make mistakes," or, "Sh*t happens!" Others are just like you. What phrases remind you that you're not the first mom to struggle, and you won't be the last?

_____

_____

_____

_____

_____

_____

_____

_____

# WHAT DOESN'T KILL YOU
# MAKES YOU STRONGER

To have gotten this far in life, you must have faced challenges. Write about a time you successfully overcame an obstacle.

_____

_____

_____

_____

    What is something you learned or gained from that experience? How might that help you as a mom?

_____

_____

_____

_____

# THE MOTHERLODE

What are some of the positives that you might realize from the challenges of motherhood you're facing right now? Did you know you could care so deeply? Did you know you could dig so deep emotionally and physically? And that you could do so much on so little sleep?

_____

_____

_____

_____

_____

_____

_____

_____

## LOVING-KINDNESS

Find a comfortable seat. Relax your body, and take a few deep breaths.

TIP: You can record and listen to yourself reading the words that follow, or find online recordings in the Resources section (page 154).

Think of someone you love, someone who makes you happy just thinking about them. It may be your baby, a pet, a friend, or a family member. Imagine them in front of you, and notice the good feelings that arise in your body and heart. You may feel warm and smile as you think of them. You care dearly for them, so imagine you can send your good feelings and good wishes to them. Words can help these good feelings grow. Say to them, "May you be safe and protected. May you be free from stress. May you know you are loved. May you know your goodness." Add any other good wishes you like. Notice how it feels and if images, color, or light come to mind as you send these wishes.

Now imagine that this loved one turns to you and gives you the same good wishes. Open your heart to receive their care. They say, "May you [meaning you] be safe and protected. May you be free from stress. May you know you are loved. May you know your goodness." Breathe in and out, taking in the love as best you can.

Now see if you can wish these things for yourself–send them to yourself from yourself. "May I be safe and protected. May I be free from stress. May I know I am loved. May I know my own goodness," and whatever else you'd like to add. Allow whatever you feel to be here. Let your experience be just as it is.

# REFLECTION

Referring to the previous exercise, "Loving-Kindness," think about what it was like for you to send and receive these good wishes. Were you able to take it in? Sometimes we're not, and that's okay. Practice being patient and kind to yourself, whatever you felt. This is a process of planting seeds, so don't be concerned if you can't see yet what will grow from them. Explore in writing what the experience was like for you.

_____

_____

_____

_____

_____

_____

_____

_____

When you care about yourself,
you take care of yourself.

—SHAUNA SHAPIRO

# MAGIC WORDS

Certain words can make each of us feel really seen, valued, and validated. Words like, "You're a good mom," "I appreciate you," and, "I love you," are some. Write about the words you wish to hear that touch your heart and fill you with peace.

_____

_____

_____

_____

_____

_____

_____

_____

_____

# MAKE YOUR OWN MAGIC

Rewrite the words from the previous page. They might be words like, "I know I'm a good mom," "I appreciate myself," or, "I love myself."

_____

_____

_____

_____

_____

_____

_____

_____

_____

## SHOWER YOURSELF WITH LOVE

Once you've written the words that mean so much to you, close your eyes and repeat them to yourself over and over. Offer yourself some comforting touch. Shower yourself with these kind words. Breathe. Allow the words to sink in.

## THE DREAM TEAM

Using your imagination, recruit your compassionate Dream Team. Pick five of the most caring, wise, encouraging, inspiring people or characters you know. Imagine that these five beings make up an inner committee of compassion. They're there for you when you're feeling bad or when things aren't going your way. Notice how it feels when you know you have them in your corner. Draw them in this space with their compassionate qualities.

# REFLECTION

How does it feel to have the Dream Team in your corner?

_____

_____

_____

_____

_____

_____

_____

_____

_____

_____

## A LOVING FRIEND

TIP: You can record and listen to yourself reading the words below or find online recordings in the Resources section (page 154).

Breathe deeply and offer yourself some comforting touch. Visualize yourself in a peaceful, safe, and comfortable place. It could be a real place, like in front of a cozy fireplace with a blanket, or somewhere you've imagined, like floating in the middle of the sea. Whatever images come to you, imagine all the sights, smells, and textures of this place, and make yourself comfortable here in your mind. When you're ready, a friendly presence is coming to visit you. This being is kind, wise, and trustworthy, knows you really well, and loves you unconditionally. This friend could be an animal, a person from your life, a spiritual being, or even a presence of light or color. Invite them into your peaceful place, and imagine them with you in as much detail as possible. They care about you and want you to be free from suffering. They know exactly what you're going through as a person and as a mother—without you saying anything to them—and they see it with wisdom and compassion. They want you to know something important, and it's exactly what you need to hear in this moment of your life. Pause and listen to their message.

Having this friend with you feels comforting and safe. Is there anything you want to say to them? They listen deeply and understand you.

This loving friend wants you to have a gift—something to remind you of their friendship and their message. Put out your hands to receive it.

Finally, just rest and enjoy their company.

# REFLECT

Referring to the previous exercise, what message did your loving friend want you to know? After writing it down, say it out loud to yourself.

_____

_____

_____

_____

_____

_____

_____

_____

_____

_____

# REFLECT

---

What is it like to be able to say anything to them and to be understood and accepted?

_____

_____

_____

_____

_____

_____

_____

_____

_____

## THE GIFT

What gift, if any, did your loving friend give you, and what does it mean to you? Can you draw the gift here?

I DESERVE TO RECEIVE
MY OWN INNER WISDOM
AND COMPASSION,
JUST LIKE EVERYONE ELSE.
I AM MY CONSTANT
COMPANION, AND I
CAN BE MY BEST FRIEND.

One thing is for sure—
you will make mistakes.
Learn to learn from them.
Learn to forgive yourself.
Learn to laugh when
everything falls apart because,
sometimes, it will.

–VIRONIKA TUGALEVA

# FACE AND FORGIVE YOUR INNER CRITIC

You know that voice inside? The one ready to point out all your faults the moment something goes wrong? That's your Inner Critic. We all have one. Usually the Inner Critic is developed to protect or motivate us in some way, but its delivery is so harsh that we just feel down, isolate ourselves, and think we're no good.

We're human. We make mistakes, we're not perfect, and sometimes we fail. The Inner Critic judges us for these natural qualities and tries to convince us that these parts of ourselves are unacceptable—that we should "do more" and "be better." This kind of thinking disconnects us from our shared, perfectly imperfect humanity.

Since you became a mom, your Inner Critic may have a lot to say. When we take on a new challenge (like parenting) and care deeply about doing it well, we strive, and criticism usually pops up. This section offers new ways to meet your Inner Critic and use its intention for good, and let go of the rest. Parenting is hard enough without beating yourself up!

# MAYBE YOU'RE NOT SO SURE ABOUT ALL THIS . . .

Self-compassion sounds nice, but many people are actually wary of the concept. They wonder, *Does it mean I won't hold myself accountable? Will I become lazy?* For some, it sounds too cheesy or soft; others doubt whether they're deserving. Often these concerns are coming from our Inner Critic, and it's important to address them. What doubts do you have about self-compassion?

_____

_____

_____

_____

_____

_____

Can you honor your doubts and also commit to trying this self-compassion process with openness for now?

## HAVE YOUR OWN BACK

Take some deep breaths, snuggle up with a soft blanket, and look around your space right now. Do what you need to do to feel safe and comfortable, especially when opening yourself up to facing your Critic. Be kind to yourself, as if you're the mother you need right now. Before you begin, offer yourself some comforting touch, and repeat what your Compassionate Voice wants you to know. (Refer to the exercise and reflection on pages 72 to 73.)

# HEARING YOUR INNER CRITIC

We must learn to be mindful and aware of when the Inner Critic is present if we want to change how its negativity affects us. It might present as a self-judgment, it may be a controlling command, or it may be highlighting our worst fears. I invite you to write about three negative messages your Critic tends to say about you as a new mom. When you finish, remind yourself that the Critic is not telling the "truth"—it is just one (negative) perspective.

The controlling part of me says: _____

_____

The judgmental part of me says: _____

_____

The fearful part of me says: _____

_____

# FACING THE CRITIC

Since you became a mom, your Inner Critic may have evolved to nitpick you in new ways about anything from your appearance, to how your baby eats or sleeps to how (not) clean your house is, and so on. What new criticisms have popped up? Write about each of them using the following prompts.

Who says you have to live up to these ideas?

_____

_____

What are your concerns if you don't?

_____

_____

_____

Are those concerns true?

_____

_____

# DEAR BODY

Our bodies support and sustain us. They are amazing and deserve love and respect. Use this space to write a letter of genuine appreciation for your one and only body.

Dear Body,

Thank you for . . .

_____

_____

_____

_____

_____

_____

_____

_____

_____

## GOOD ENOUGH IS ENOUGH

One way inner criticism shows up is by downplaying our accomplishments. Notice when you say to yourself or others, "Anyone could have done that," or, "I could do more, or better." This minimizing mindset is present for many moms. Remember, just because moms have done this work throughout history does not make it less worthy of acknowledgment, praise, and pride! List three things you're doing fine as a mom. It may not be "perfect," but it *is* good enough!

1. _____

   _____

2. _____

   _____

3. _____

   _____

# RELEASE MOM SHAME

What have you not told anyone about your experience as a new mom? Offer yourself some comforting touch and deep breaths as you reflect and write.

_____

_____

_____

_____

What keeps you from sharing these thoughts or feelings?

_____

_____

_____

_____

# BE HONEST

How do you respond to the statement, "It's okay to not love being a mom every second"?

_____

_____

_____

_____

_____

_____

_____

_____

_____

## SEE THE INNER CRITIC MORE CLEARLY

The Inner Critic can show up in many ways for different people. Your Inner Critic may be a voice, a tone, a physical sensation, or an emotion. In this exercise, I invite you to get familiar with how your Critic shows up for you by drawing your experience of it. Artistic skills are not required! Take a moment now to remember a time when you were hard on yourself. Then, just using colors, lines, and shapes, go ahead and doodle your expression of the Inner Critic here:

Once your drawing feels complete, give your Critic a name. (Be as literal or as silly as you like!)

# ARGUE WITH YOUR INNER CRITIC

What would your Dream Team say to the Critic? What about your Compassionate Voice? And what would your friends say?

_____

_____

_____

_____

_____

_____

_____

_____

_____

What we don't need
in the midst of struggle is
shame for being human.

–BRENÉ BROWN

# THE SELF-IMPROVEMENT TRAP

Perfection and self-improvement can be the Inner Critic in disguise. Wishing we were different than we are is a common way we suffer. Consider the ways we let comparison rob us of the beauty of what we have now.

In what ways do you compare yourself to your past self (even though you have many more responsibilities and way less time now)?

_____

_____

In what ways do you compare yourself to other moms on social media or in real life, even if you only see a (sometimes staged and filtered) snapshot?

_____

_____

In what ways do you compare yourself to some imagined "perfect mom" or other ideal?

_____

_____

# PERFECTLY IMPERFECT

If you feel criticized for your imperfections, take some time here to write about any silver linings that may emerge from these perceived flaws. Do your imperfections add to your humor? Connection with others? Forgiveness of others? Does it help you focus on what you truly value? Explore here.

_____

_____

_____

_____

_____

_____

_____

_____

## CALMING BREATH

When we exhale for longer than we inhale, it helps us feel more calm. Give yourself some comforting touch, then count to four as you inhale, and exhale as you count to eight. Repeat for 10 cycles of breath, doing your best to focus only on counting and on how the breath feels in your body.

# HEY, INNER CRITIC, LET'S TALK

Critic, is there something you're trying to protect me from?

_____

_____

_____

Let the Critic know its impact on you. How does it feel to be the one who's criticized? Is it working the way the Critic intended?

_____

_____

Can you offer any appreciation to the Critic for any of its good intentions (even though its methods are misguided)?

_____

_____

_____

_____

# A NEW PERSPECTIVE

Now that the Critic has been heard, ask it to make space for a compassionate perspective. What does your Compassionate Voice say? If you need a reminder, you can revisit your Loving Friend (page 72).

_____

_____

_____

_____

_____

_____

_____

_____

_____

_____

## CHANGE YOUR RELATIONSHIP TO YOUR CRITIC

Is there anything you'd like to add to your drawing of the Inner Critic (page 88)? Perhaps something to signify a new boundary, appreciation, or understanding, or a demotion in status on your internal committee?

_____

_____

_____

_____

# IT'S OKAY TO OUTGROW YOUR CRITIC

As you become more familiar with how your Inner Critic shows up in you, does it remind you of anyone from your life? Many people first heard these messages as children from family members, teachers, coaches, or other important figures. Write about when you first heard these criticisms. You may still hear the Critic, but you don't have to identify with it or believe it.

# DO YOU HAVE AN OUTER CRITIC?

It can be devastating to hear direct or indirect critiques of how we are parenting. This can bring up defensiveness, anger, sadness, and shame. Those feelings are difficult to bear. If someone in your life is criticizing you—as a mom or otherwise—how can your Compassionate Voice and your Dream Team of support help you care for and stand up for yourself?

_____

_____

_____

_____

_____

_____

_____

_____

_____

_____

# TAKE CARE OF LITTLE YOU

Even in the best of circumstances, our needs as children were not always met. What do you wish you'd had more of as a child?

_____

_____

_____

_____

    Can you offer that to yourself now, with some kind words, a gentle tone, or comforting touch?

_____

_____

_____

_____

# MOTHER YOURSELF

If you could be a mom to yourself as a child or as you are now, what would you do or say?

_____

_____

_____

_____

_____

_____

_____

## EVICT THE INNER CRITIC

It's normal to have critical thoughts, but we don't need to believe them or give them our undivided attention. Sometimes these thoughts and feelings simply need acknowledgment and a place to go. Imagine that you can place the Inner Critic and its opinions somewhere at a safe distance from you. Use this space to draw a place or container for your critical thoughts to chill out (and maybe even move on) once they're seen and heard.

I AM PERFECTLY
IMPERFECT, AND
I AM THE BEST
MOTHER FOR
MY CHILD.

The greatness of a
community is most accurately
measured by the compassionate
actions of its members.

–CORETTA SCOTT KING

# SHOWER OTHERS WITH EMPATHY

We're all in this together. Self-compassion is not meant to be practiced in isolation—it's about creating a community of acceptance. Seeing ourselves and others (especially our partners and support people) in a compassionate light is a virtuous cycle of forgiveness and kindness. This outlook paves the way for connection to something greater than ourselves. You're now part of a long legacy of mothers who have come before you, who fiercely loved and nurtured every human being who has ever lived. When you are loving toward and accepting of yourself, you're honoring the wholehearted work of all mothers.

As we practice compassion for ourselves, we see everyone's strengths and vulnerabilities more clearly and kindly, and our connection to humankind deepens. We have much more in common than what separates us, and focusing on our shared humanity helps us feel less alone, more forgiving, and more accepting of ourselves and others. By connecting with our communities, we nurture a felt sense of belonging, imperfections and all.

# BREATH CONNECTS US ALL

TIP: Guided practice recordings can be found in the Resources section (page 154).

It can be hard to feel connected to others when you're so busy and adjusting to life as a mom. When others you care for need support, it may feel overwhelming to you. You may not know what to do or say when someone else is struggling, or the demands of your life right now may keep you isolated. This practice helps you stay connected in your heart by using your breath.

Sit comfortably and supported, and notice your natural rhythm of breathing. Feel the air coming in and enlivening the body, and feel the relaxation as air moves out. As you breathe in, imagine inhaling self-compassion and kindness. Using those words, or others, such as "love," "caring," or "peace," focus on breathing in these qualities and wishes for yourself for 10 inhales.

Now think of someone you care for who is needing some compassion. As you breathe out, imagine exhaling good wishes and words of care and encouragement to that person.

Continue breathing in compassion for yourself and breathing out compassion for the other. As you do this, images of color or light may form; just notice what comes up, and allow it as you let the compassion flow from you to them and back again. Breathe like this for a few minutes, feeling that you're connected.

# REFLECTION

How does it feel to connect to others using your breath?

_____

_____

_____

_____

_____

_____

_____

_____

## COMPASSION FOR ALL MOMS

You're a member of the Mom Club, and it's a mighty one. Consider how many mothers are in your neighborhood, city, and country—and the world. Moms are everywhere, and once a mom, always a mom.

Using the same compassionate breathing skills you just practiced, can you breathe in compassion for yourself, and breathe out compassion for all moms everywhere? Breathe compassion for all moms who worry about their children, who don't have enough support, who are working so hard, and who never feel like it's enough.

Take your time breathing in for you, and then, on your exhale, send your compassionate breath to all the moms you know. Breathe in for you, and then exhale compassion for the moms in your neighborhood. Expand your reach every few breaths, including more and more moms, sending them understanding, kindness, and compassion.

# HEY, SIS!

How does it feel to recognize that you're a member of this sisterhood of mothers? How does it feel to connect with them using your breath?

_____

_____

_____

_____

_____

_____

_____

_____

## FEELING COMPASSION: PART 1

TIP: Guided practice recordings can be found in the Resources section (page 154).

Think of a mom you admire, and imagine that she's right in front of you. Breathe in for yourself and out for her.

Give yourself some comforting touch as you think of this person and the weight she carries as a mother. Consider the stress and hardships she has endured, as everyone does at some point in their lives.

As a mom, she has felt more vulnerability, love, and pride than can be measured. She is filled with strength—some that has been shown and more that has yet to be seen. Without even knowing the details, you can know for certain this mom has experienced pain, doubt, anxiety, and disappointment. She has made sacrifices and felt lost.

Do you feel a desire to reassure or comfort this other mom? Recognize that this feeling is compassion.

## FEELING COMPASSION: PART 2

TIP: Guided practice recordings can be found in the Resources section (page 154).

Find a mirror and look at yourself with kindness, as if greeting a friend. Hello, dear one! Offer yourself some comforting touch, and breathe in and out with care.

Just by virtue of being human, and being a mother, you have endured stress and hardships, as everyone does at some point in their lives. As a mother, you have likely felt more vulnerability, love, and pride than can be measured. You're filled with strength—some that has been shown, and more that has yet to be seen. You've likely experienced pain, doubt, anxiety, and disappointment. You've made sacrifices and sometimes felt lost.

This is what it's like to be a mother.

Do you feel a desire to reassure or comfort yourself? This feeling is self-compassion. If you feel something else, can you be kind and curious about those feelings?

# REFLECTION

What is it like to consider that a mother you admire also carries difficulty with her?

_____

_____

_____

_____

What was it like to see yourself in this way, with strength and vulnerability? Did you feel self-compassion or something else?

_____

_____

_____

_____

# NOTICE COMPARISONS

What do we compare with other moms? We don't always talk about it, but the list is there. We compare how we feed our babies, the birthing experience, how our bodies look, our age, how we relate to our partners, whether we work outside the home, whether we have childcare, where and when the baby sleeps, how much the baby cries—the list goes on and on. Use these writing prompts to explore how you compare yourself to others. Be really honest—this is just for you!

I feel better than other moms when I compare:

_____

_____

_____

I feel worse than other moms when I compare:

_____

_____

_____

## COMPARISON IS THE THIEF OF JOY

Notice what feelings you had as you completed each comparison—perhaps pity, superiority, inferiority, or shame? It's completely natural to compare, and it's impossible not to notice differences. However, living in comparison will ultimately leave you feeling isolated. Whether you deem your situation or approach better or worse than others', as long as you remain in a judgmental mindset (hello, Inner Critic!), you'll separate yourself from the tribe of mamas and get caught up in a mom-shaming culture. Trust that every mother (including you!) is doing the best she can. Say out loud to yourself, "We are all doing the best we can!"

# WHAT MAKES CHARACTER?

Our imperfections make us whole, real people. Think of a time when someone's "imperfections" made you like them even more, and write about how you felt being around them.

_____

_____

_____

_____

_____

_____

_____

_____

_____

## HEAR OTHERS' STORIES

Read real accounts of life as a new mom. Find books, essays, or social media accounts that are genuine in showing the struggles and joys of this time of life. As you do this, try not to compare, but focus on the wide variety of experiences that are all valid.

TIP: Check out the Resources section of this book for some ideas (page 154).

## FIND YOUR PEOPLE!

One of the best things you can do for yourself and the community is to join or start a moms' group. Sometimes this happens organically, but often you'll need to put yourself out there—text a friend of a friend who just had a baby, post on social media, or search for parent groups to join through local organizations. Ideally, you can meet regularly and face-to-face. It's so important to connect with other first-time moms. You'll help each other navigate the unknowns together. Sharing your experience with others who are "in it" at the same time as you is empowering and healing.

# SHARE WHAT YOU'VE LEARNED

Now that you're a mom, what advice would you give expectant moms and other first-time moms?

_____

_____

_____

How does it feel to know what you know now? How would it feel to help others with this knowledge?

_____

_____

_____

Do you know someone you could pass on this advice to?

_____

_____

_____

Be kinder to yourself.
And then let your kindness
flood the world.

—PEMA CHODRON

# COMPASSION IN YOUR RELATIONSHIP

Don't keep score. Remember, if you have a partner, they're doing a lot, too (yes, yes, you may be doing more, but we're not here to compare)! Both of you are doing a lot more than ever before, and it's a big change. Try to put yourself in their shoes, and write out five of the challenges they are facing as a new parent.

1. _____

_____

2. _____

_____

3. _____

_____

4. _____

_____

5. _____

_____

# YOU'RE SO GREAT BECAUSE . . .

Make a list of five things you appreciate about your partner or support person, especially now that you have a child.

1. _____

_____

2. _____

_____

3. _____

_____

4. _____

_____

5. _____

_____

## SHARE THE LOVE

I invite you to share something from the last two writing prompts with your partner. Let them know you see their strengths and the challenges they struggle with, and you care.

# IT TAKES A VILLAGE

Hopefully, you have felt supported by others during your journey to become a mom, and now that your little one has arrived. Even if your support network isn't how you imagined it would be, take some time to appreciate the support you have, just as it is.

Write a letter to those who are there for you, letting them know what it means to have their support.

Dear . . .

_____

_____

_____

_____

_____

_____

_____

# COMPASSION FOR
# YOUR OWN MOM

Now that you're a mom, how has your perspective shifted about your mother? Explore in writing how being a mom yourself has changed how you think or feel about your mother. Look for ways to tap into any new care and compassion for her.

_____

_____

_____

_____

_____

_____

_____

_____

## BOOK CLUB

Consider starting a book club with this journal. It's more likely you'll stay engaged in this new self-compassionate approach to life with the support of a compassionate community, especially if you mark it on your calendar. It feels good to connect to other moms, turning moments of struggle into moments of deep connection.

## LEAN INTO THE COMMUNITY OF VETERAN PARENTS

You'll find online groups for local parents wherever you are, and they're an endless resource. Sign up for parenting newsletters or meetups, or just join the online discussion boards for your neighborhood or region. This can help you with anything from finding a great pediatrician to getting secondhand baby gear. Other parents are often happy to share information, emotional support, and tangible help.

I'M PART OF A STRONG, SUPPORTIVE PARENTING COMMUNITY. WE'RE DOING THE BEST WE CAN, AND WE DON'T HAVE TO DO IT ALONE.

Self-compassion
is like a muscle. The more
we practice flexing it,
especially when life doesn't
go exactly according to plan
(a frequent scenario for most of us),
the stronger and more resilient
our compassion muscle becomes.

–SHARON SALZBERG

# NURTURE YOUR SELF-COMPASSION EVERY DAY

Keep up the good work! Being a mother will continue to be the best and hardest thing you do, and being kind and compassionate to yourself will help you savor the good and rise to the challenges ahead.

Whenever you're compassionate to yourself, you're modeling self-love for your child, who will learn that we're *all* worthy of love, kindness, and compassion—even when we're not "perfect," when we make mistakes, or if we struggle in some way. Support yourself in making this meaningful change by weaving self-compassion into your life in simple and easy ways.

This section offers tools to help you create a more self-compassionate future for yourself and your family. You'll feel better, and that will motivate you to maintain it—but keep in mind that it also takes mindful intention and practice.

Whenever you feel you've faltered, remember that you can simply begin again.

## FIND THE GOOD

When you haven't slept more than three straight hours for months, things can look bleak. While nothing can replace a restful night's sleep, you can cultivate a perspective that seeks out the good and really enjoys what it finds.

Next time you're with your little one, let your attention linger on the beauty of your child. Stare into their wise eyes, feel the buttery softness of their skin, and marvel at the cuteness of their tiny toes and fingers. Do so with the intention that appreciating and enjoying this moment to its fullest is good for you, and it's priming your mind to seek out what makes you happy.

It's self-fulfilling: If you practice mindfulness of joy and beauty, you'll experience even more joy and beauty.

# EXPANDING THE GOOD

What moments with your baby do you naturally soak in with appreciation? Notice how, through writing, you can appreciate these things in your mind and heart even when your baby isn't right here.

_____

_____

_____

_____

_____

_____

_____

_____

_____

_____

## SAVOR RIGHT NOW

Look around your space now. Feel the seat beneath you, listen, and feel your breath inside your body. Using your senses, notice three simple things you can savor with gratitude, comfort, amusement, or joy.

# NO ONE DOES IT ALONE

Think about the people in your life who have helped you grow into the person you are today. What qualities have others helped foster in you that you appreciate about yourself?

_____

_____

_____

_____

_____

_____

_____

After you've written, soak in any feelings of warmth, pride, or gratitude. Practice appreciating these qualities in yourself and how they connect you to others.

# WHAT'S WORKING FOR YOU?

What has made this journal experience work best for you? Does this journal give you a reason to make time for yourself? Do you doodle in the margins? Do you enjoy a cup of tea while you journal? Is there anything you'd like to keep doing to help give yourself this gift of self-reflection and self-compassion? Making this process feel good is important. Brainstorm here on what's worked so far and what else you might do.

_____

_____

_____

_____

_____

_____

_____

_____

# IN THE MOMENT

What can you do *in the moment*? Perhaps offering yourself some comforting touch when you can't sleep, a smile when you catch your reflection in the mirror, or a friendly breath right before you feed your baby? What self-compassionate acts can you do in your everyday life? Make a list of at least five things you can do on a regular day that are infused with self-compassion.

1. _____

_____

2. _____

_____

3. _____

_____

4. _____

_____

5. _____

_____

Speak quietly to yourself and promise there will be better days. Whisper gently to yourself and provide assurance that you really are extending your best effort. Console your bruised and tender spirit with reminders of many other successes. Offer comfort in practical and tangible ways—as if you were encouraging your dearest friend. Recognize that on certain days the greatest grace is that the day is over and you get to close your eyes. Tomorrow comes more brightly.

—MARY ANNE RADMACHER

## LOOKING AHEAD . . .

TIP: Guided practice recordings can be found in the Resources section (page 154).

Imagine that your child is all grown up. Maybe you even have grandchildren. You're much older now, and reflecting on your life. You sit somewhere peaceful with a beautiful, expansive view. Picture it in your mind now and take a deep breath. You feel deeply content because you know you lived a life guided by your most important values. Savor this satisfaction.

# WHAT REALLY MATTERS

Reflecting on the previous exercise, what values guided your life that felt so satisfying? Some examples of values are honesty, friendship, hard work, kindness, creativity, loyalty, nature, and courage.

TIP: A values list and exercise can be found in the Resources section (page 154).

_____

_____

_____

_____

What things did you do to live in alignment with your values?

_____

_____

_____

_____

_____

# WHAT GETS IN THE WAY?

What internal and external barriers sometimes keep you from living out your values? Remember to be kind to yourself as you acknowledge these obstacles.

_____

_____

_____

_____

_____

_____

_____

_____

_____

# TRY SOME KINDNESS

If you could overcome some barriers, even just partly, how might you do that with kindness and compassion for yourself?

_____

_____

_____

_____

If the barriers cannot be overcome, write some words of understanding for yourself and the circumstances.

_____

_____

_____

_____

# SET AN INTENTION

Make a commitment to yourself. Write a promise to yourself about how you'd like to live a life that is more connected to your values. Keep your intention focused on wanting the best for yourself, not as a demand or self-criticism.

    I promise . . .

_____

_____

_____

_____

_____

_____

_____

_____

_____

# BE A MAMA BEAR

Practice setting boundaries for yourself, just as you do for your little one. One of the gifts of becoming a mom is that it helps you clarify your values and priorities, and let go of some guilt because you know you're doing what's best for your family. *This is fierce compassion.* Doing what's best for you is also what's best for your family! If you're protecting your baby's naptime or mealtime and limiting their exposure to criticism and unkind people, try to include yourself in that.

Use this space to brainstorm some ways you can set boundaries for yourself. Moms need to eat, rest, and recharge, too—and you don't have to invest time in people who bring you down.

_____

_____

_____

_____

_____

_____

_____

# DO LESS!

It may seem like practicing self-compassion is yet another item on your ever-growing list of responsibilities and things to do—but keep in mind that self-compassion is guided by what's best for *you*. An act of self-compassion may take no time at all, and it might actually save you time. Self-compassion often means saying no. Moms have a tendency to take on too much and not realize it until later (if ever!). Saying no may trigger feelings of guilt, but you truly haven't done anything wrong. Write down a few things that you could say no to. Would this free up some of your time and emotional energy?

_____

_____

_____

_____

_____

_____

_____

# MOTIVATE YOURSELF WITH LOVE

If you're stuck in thinking or behavior that's not in your best interest, something in your life may really need to change. Self-compassion is about wanting the best for yourself, and this can be done with fierce compassion. What's best for you may mean changing parts of your lifestyle because you're worth it, and you deserve to feel better and live your values. We often try to motivate ourselves with criticism, but that's not very effective long term. Let's explore how to change with compassion.

Write about a behavior you would like to change: _____

Imagine your wise, compassionate Dream Team is here. Why would they want this change for you?

_____

_____

What small steps would they suggest to help you move toward your goal? How would they encourage you? Notice how it feels to have a plan founded on self-kindness.

_____

_____

# A LITTLE HELP

Self-compassion asks, "What do I need?" What new moms need is help and support. Write a letter to your partner or a support person about your needs. Try to
be as specific as possible without feeling self-conscious. Your needs are valid.

---

---

---

---

---

---

---

---

---

## IT NEVER HURTS TO ASK

Share this letter or have a conversation with your partner or support person about what you need and how they can best help you. You may not always get what you ask for, but how will you know unless you try? Heads-up: When you do get help, keep in mind that your partner may not do things exactly the way you would, and that's okay. Remember to breathe.

## LOOK AT ALL YOU'VE LEARNED!

Reflect on the practices that were most helpful for you, and use the space below to jot down any notes for yourself. Then, go back through the journal and dog-ear the writing prompts that were most meaningful and that you may want to respond to again.

\
\
\
\
\
\
\
\

## REMEMBERING SELF-COMPASSION

What messages of self-compassion would you like to install in your heart and mind as a new mom? How can you remind yourself of these messages daily? Maybe you could put a note on your bathroom mirror or set a reminder on your calendar. Take a moment now to put these reminders in your life. Go ahead, I'll wait.

_____

_____

_____

_____

# OH, THANK YOU, ME!

Write a letter of gratitude to yourself for engaging in this journal. You may not have done every exercise, and that's okay! Honor what you have done for yourself. Caring for yourself and taking care of yourself are so important.

_____

_____

_____

_____

_____

_____

_____

_____

_____

I'M CULTIVATING A
NEW, KINDER WAY
TO CARE FOR MYSELF THAT
WILL BENEFIT ME AND
ALL THOSE AROUND ME.
IT WILL TAKE PRACTICE,
AND I AM WORTH IT.

# A FINAL WORD

Here we are at the end of this journal, but it's just the start of your self-compassion journey. You have made it this far, which means your little one is that much older and bigger, and you are that much further along in the adventure of being a mom. This is a lifelong practice. As you've seen, you and your child will grow quickly.

Things will keep changing, as is the natural course of life. No matter how much things change, the key ingredients to self-compassion will remain the same: Continue to pause and notice how you're feeling, recognize when you're struggling, see how it's a part of your humanity, and offer yourself kindness. The more you practice, the better you'll feel. Keep in mind that the goal is not to be free from tough feelings or experiences—those are natural parts of human life. Instead, it's about moving through those difficulties with less resistance and more ease.

An important piece of advice: Be self-compassionate about your self-compassion practice. You won't be compassionate 100 percent of the time. If you notice self-judgment creeping in, remember a couple of things. (1) It's great that you noticed! That awareness will help you hit pause on the automatic ways that you cope with stress and choose how you want to respond. (2) It's an opportunity to be kind to yourself about a lapse in compassion. We're human, and old habits die hard. Practicing self-compassion is a relief from our habitual ways. It may still feel foreign to you to offer yourself kindness through touch, a gentle tone, and loving words, but it will become more familiar with repetition.

It can feel revolutionary to live with self-compassion in our world. Surround yourself with compassion. Seek out other moms who reflect authenticity, kindness, and understanding back to you. What you're doing for yourself will benefit your child(ren) and your family, and it will ripple compassion out into the world.

I wish you kindness, forgiveness, acceptance, peace, and ease.

YOU GOT THIS.

# RESOURCES

## GUIDED MEDITATIONS

**Guided Self-Compassion Meditations to Accompany This Journal by Hanna Kreiner**
HannaKreiner.com/meditations

**Meditations for Parents by Yael Shy**
Sonima.com/meditation/advice-for-new-moms

**Mindful Self-Compassion Meditations**
CenterforMSC.org/practice-msc/guided-meditations-and-exercises

**RAIN: Recognize, Allow, Investigate, Nurture by Tara Brach**
TaraBrach.com/meditation-practice-rain

**Self-Compassion Meditations to Release Self-Criticism and Foster Self-Kindness: Powerful Guided Imagery to Nurture Self-Love, Self-Appreciation, and Self-Respect by Traci Stein and Health Journeys**
HealthJourneys.com/self-compassion-meditations-to-release-self-criticism -and-foster-self-kindness

# SOCIAL MEDIA RESOURCES

@drcassidy

@mothercarejourney

#motherhoodunfiltered

@neffselfcompassion

@parentselfcare

@selfcompassioncommunity

# PODCASTS

*Happy as a Mother*

*Holding Space*

*The Longest Shortest Time*

*The Mom Hour*

*Motherhood Sessions*

*Woke Mommy Chatter*

# WEBSITES

**Postpartum Support International: Postpartum.net**
PSI helps families with postpartum depression, anxiety, and distress by providing information, offering online support groups, and connecting people to local specialists through a directory of psychotherapists and psychiatrists. Keep in mind that birthing and adoptive mothers and fathers experience postpartum mood disorders. PSI Helpline: (800) 944-4PPD (4773)

**Self-Compassion.org**
Kristin Neff, PhD, is a leading researcher of self-compassion. Her site offers exercises, guided meditations, and information on her research.

**Self-Compassion Test: CenterforMSC.org/take-the-self-compassion-test**
Completing this research-validated questionnaire will give you insight into how self-compassionate you are. Your responses are broken down by the different components of self-compassion, which can guide you on where to focus your practice.

**Values Card Sort: MotivationalInterviewing.org/sites/default/files/valuescardsort_0.pdf**
These printable values cards can be sorted in order of importance for you.

## WORKSHOPS

**Center for Mindful Self-Compassion: CenterforMSC.org**
Founded by leading researchers on self-compassion, this resource connects you to evidence-based Mindful Self-Compassion classes, workshops, trainings, and retreats. It also provides live online guided meditations and at-home practices to support your continued practice.

**Community of Mindful Parenting: CommunityofMindfulParenting.com**
An online community for parents and extended families interested in raising children with mindfulness to improve family relationships. This community offers online and local classes for parents and caregivers. Their program, *Listening Mothers*, is designed for moms of babies 0 to 6 months old.

**The Gottman Method: Gottman.com/parents**
John and Julie Gottman have developed programs for couples based on decades of research. This site links to *Bringing Baby Home* workshops, *Transition to Parenthood* courses, books, and more.

**Mindful Compassionate Parenting: MedSchool.ucsd.edu/som/ fmph/research/mindfulness/programs/youth-family/Pages/ Mindful-Parenting.aspx**
Mindful Compassionate Parenting is a course that teaches parents and care-taker the art of being fully present with your child with kindness, consideration, and compassion.

## POSTNATAL YOGA CLASSES

**Om Births: OmBirths.com/online-postnatal-yoga-program**
Postnatal and mommy and baby yoga, as well as online community gatherings for new mothers.

**Whole Mama Yoga: WholeMamaYoga.com**
Live and pre-recorded online postnatal yoga classes to connect with other new moms while caring for yourself through movement, breathing, and community.

# BOOKS

*And Baby Makes Three* by Julie Gottman and John Gottman

*Fierce Self-Compassion: How Women Can Harness Kindness to Speak Up, Claim Their Power, and Thrive* by Kristin Neff

*The Gifts of Imperfect Parenting: Raising Children with Courage, Compassion, and Connection* by Brené Brown

*Lovingkindness: The Revolutionary Art of Happiness* by Sharon Salzberg

*The Mindful Path to Self-Compassion: Freeing Yourself from Destructive Thoughts and Emotions* by Christopher Germer

*Parenting from the Inside Out: How a Deeper Self-Understanding Can Help You Raise Children Who Thrive* by Daniel Siegel and Mary Hartzell

*The Power of Showing Up: How Parental Presence Shapes Who Our Kids Become and How Their Brains Get Wired* by Daniel Siegel and Tina Payne Bryson

*Radical Acceptance: Embracing Your Life with the Heart of a Buddha* by Tara Brach

*Radical Compassion: Learning to Love Yourself and Your World with the Practice of RAIN* by Tara Brach

*Self-Compassion for Parents: Nurture Your Child by Caring for Yourself* by Susan M. Pollak

*Self-Compassion: The Proven Power of Being Kind to Yourself* by Kristin Neff

# REFERENCES

AZ Quotes. "Pema Chodron." Accessed March 20, 2021. azquotes.com
/quote/536876.

Bachman, Justin. "King's Widow Urges Acts of Compassion" *Los Angeles Times*,
Associated Press, January 17, 2000. LATimes.com/archives/la-xpm-2000-jan
-17-mn-54832-story.html

Bits of Positivity. "Best Self-Compassion and Acceptance Quotes."
Accessed April 4, 2021. BitsofPositivity.com/best-self-compassion
-self-acceptance-quotes.

Brach, Tara. *Radical Acceptance: Embracing Your Life with the Heart of a Buddha*.
New York: Bantam Books, 2003.

Doyle, Glennon. *Untamed*. New York: The Dia Press, 2020.

Germer, C., and K. D. Neff. "Mindful Self-Compassion (MSC)." *The Handbook of
Mindfulness-Based Programs: Every Established Intervention, From Medicine to
Education*, edited by Itai Itvzan, 357–367. London: Routledge, 2019.

Goodreads. "Kristin Neff Quotes." Accessed April 4, 2021. goodreads.com
/author/quotes/4559299.Kristin_Neff.

Minimalist Quotes. "What We Don't Need in The Midst of Struggle Is
Shame for Being Human." Accessed April 6, 2021. minimalistquotes.com
/brene-brown-quote-22322/.

Morrison, Toni. *Beloved*. New York: Vintage Books, 2004.

Neff, Kristin. "Exercise 2: Self-Compassion Break." Self-Compassion. Accessed
    March 30, 2021. Self-Compassion.org/exercise-2-self-compassion-break.

Neff, Kristin, and Christopher Germer. *The Mindful Self-Compassion Workbook:
    A Proven Way to Accept Yourself, Build Inner Strength and Thrive*. New York: The
    Guilford Press, 2018.

Neff, Kristin, and Christopher Germer. *Teaching the Mindful Self-Compassion
    Program: A Guide for Professionals*. New York: The Guilford Press, 2019.

Raphael, Dana. *The Tender Gift: Breastfeeding*. Hoboken: Prentice Hall, 1973.

Real Food - Whole Life. "134 The Secret to More Calm, Clarity & Joy: Redefining
    Mindfulness & Self-Compassion With Shauna Shapiro, Ph.D." Accessed March
    25, 2021. RealFoodWholeLife.com/feelgoodeffect/redefining-mindfulness
    -shauna-shapiro.

Ricardo, Cindy. "Silencing the Inner Critic: The Power of Self Compassion."
    GoodTherapy. Accessed March 29, 2021. GoodTherapy.org/blog
    /silencing-the-inner-critic-the-power-of-self-compassion-0608154.

Salzberg, S. *Real Love: The Art of Mindful Connection*. New York: Flatiron
    Books, 2017.

SELFFA. "134 Self-Compassion Quotes." Accessed April 21, 2021. SELFFA.com
    /self-compassion-quotes.

Solo Quotes. "Friendship Quotes: Self-Compassion." Accessed April 25, 2021.
    SoloQuotes.com/life/friendship/friendship-quotes-self-compassion.

Stellar, J. E., and D. Keltner. "Compassion." *Handbook of Positive Emotions*, edited
    by M. M. Tugade, M. N. Shiota, & L. D. Kirby, 329–341. New York: The Guilford
    Press, 2014.

Trudeau, Michelle. "Human Connections Start with a Friendly Touch." NPR, September 20, 2010. NPR.org/templates/story/story .php?storyId=128795325.

Tugaleva, Vironika. *The Art of Talking to Yourself.* Soulux Press, 2017.

# ACKNOWLEDGMENTS

Thank you to my sweet kids, Sophie and Stella, for making me a mom. A big thanks to my husband, Brian, for loving me, imperfections and all, and helping me see the world and myself as full of potential. Thank you to my parents, Meryl and Mohammed, for loving me and giving me three awesome sisters, Lena, Sommer, and Sara. I am especially grateful to my mom for teaming up with Brian to nourish and care for my family as I wrote. I am also so appreciative of the enthusiastic support of my in-laws, Stina and Joel.

I have the best friends in the world who help me see myself with more grace. When I forget how to talk to myself with fierce compassion, I know I can call on them. Special shout-out to Sarah and Bryn for their writing feedback and encouragement. I thank them and my many mentors who have taught me and helped me do what I love regardless of what my Inner Critic says.

# ABOUT THE AUTHOR

Hanna G. Kreiner, LICSW, LCSW is a licensed psychotherapist, author, and teacher of mindfulness and self-compassion. She has found mindfulness to be a strong foundation in facing life's greatest challenges with more ease. Her personal practice informs her work providing integrative psychotherapy, facilitating support groups and stress reduction workshops, guiding meditations, and teaching mindfulness and self-compassion courses. She brings warmth, humor, insight, and authenticity to her work with individual, group, and corporate clients. Learn more about Hanna's work at HannaKreiner.com.